TABLE OF CONTENTS

1. 9 EXCEL FUNCTIONS YOU WILL USE 95% OF THE TIME

SUMPRODUCT – The best function overall. As its name implies, this function multiplies and then sums ranges of cells, but its versatility goes way beyond that functionality. See below four examples of things you can do with this function.

- **Calculate a weighted average of your stocks purchase price on cell C5**, combining SUMPRODUCT with SUM: =SUMPRODUCT(B2:B3,C2:C3)/SUM(B2:B3)

	A	B	C
1	Stocks	Shares	Price
2	BAC	50	$200
3	BAC	100	$250
4			
5	Weighted Avg:		$233

- **How many GOOG shares did I purchase in March? This is SUMPRODUCT's look up functionality.** We must look up values in the table and sum them. It is more powerful than VLOOKUP and INDEX-MATCH-MATCH because they would only take the first result that meets the conditions.

  First, select the entire range of values of the table (C2:D6) and then create the three conditions we need to find and sum the right cells. You can add more than three conditions if you need to. Remember that every time you enter text such as "Shares" in your functions, you must use quotation marks.

  Formula in C8:
  =SUMPRODUCT(C2:D6*(C1:D1="Shares")*(A2:A6="GOOG")*(B2:B6="March"))

	A	B	C	D
1	Ticker	Date	Shares	Price
2	GOOG	January	50	$200
3	AMZN	April	100	$250
4	GME	February	30	$100
5	GOOG	March	10	$50
6	GOOG	March	30	$300
7				
8	GOOG Shares:		40	

4 parts in this function, all linked using *

C2:D6 → range to sum

(C1:D1="Shares") → first condition

(A2:A6="GOOG") → second condition

(B2:B6="March") → third condition

- **Count cells that meet a condition.** You are creating a report and must show YTD data based on the date in cell H1. You could use the function MATCH, but you would have to update the ranges of your formula every year. *How can you avoid this and further automate your reports?*

  Try =SUMPRODUCT(1*(A1:F1<=H1)*(YEAR(A1:F1)=YEAR(H1))). Note the expression "1*". Because SUMPRODUCT multiplies and then sums, this time it is doing 1 * the number of conditions that are TRUE, and then it sums all of them. Therefore, 1*1 + 1*1 + 1*1 = 3

  - The first condition (A1:F1<=H1) will select any dates lower or equal to H1

  - The second condition (YEAR(A1:F1)=YEAR(H1)) will select any dates where the year matches the year in H1.

  Only Jan-22, Feb-22 and Mar-22 (3 cases) meet those two conditions.

	A	B	C	D	E	F	G	H
1	Nov-21	Dec-21	Jan-22	Feb-22	Mar-22	Apr-22		Mar-22
2								3

- **What is the YTD monthly average of each item as of the date showing in cell H1?** This is an example of how to combine the previous two use cases shown: adding up and counting cells. This formula is useful to automate reports and to create dashboards where everything updates as you change your report's date.

  The formula I used in cell H2 is:
  =SUMPRODUCT(B2:E2*(B1:E1<=H1))/SUMPRODUCT(1*(B1:E1<=H1)).

	A	B	C	D	E	F	G	H
1		Jan-22	Feb-22	Mar-22	Apr-22		Choose date	Mar-22
2	Item A	40	50	10	5		Item A Avg	33.3
3	Item B	35	60	20	15		Item B Avg	38.3
4	Item C	20	25	60	30		Item C Avg	35.0

First, SUMPRODUCT(B2:E2*(B1:E1<=H1)) adds up any values from row 2 whose dates are lower or equal to H1

Then, SUMPRODUCT(1*(B1:E1<=H1)) divides by the number of months to create the YTD monthly average.

SUMIFS – This function adds up values that meet more than one condition.

How many shoes made in Spain did we sell last month?

Formula in D10 =SUMIFS(D3:D8,A3:A8,"Shoes",C3:C8,"Spain"). First choose the range of all existing values (D3:D8), then go column by column choosing the conditions you want.

If there is a column whose values do not matter for your analysis, just ignore it, like "Color" in this example.

COUNTIFS – Similar to the previous one, it counts how many times the conditions are met, instead of adding the results up.

How many types of products were made in Spain and cost over $20?

Formula in D9 =COUNTIFS(C2:C7,"Spain",D2:D7,">20").

	A	B	C	D
1	Product	Color	Country	Price
2	Shirt	Blue	France	$ 50
3	Shoes	Red	Spain	$ 15
4	Jeans	Green	USA	$ 35
5	Sandals	Black	Italy	$ 40
6	Hat	White	Spain	$ 25
7	Sweatshirt	Yellow	Canada	$ 60
8				
9				1

This is also an example on how to use logical operators such as "<", ">", "=<", "=>", "<>", "=" in your functions.

INDEX-MATCH-MATCH – This formula is a helpful solution to look up values and it is better than the legendary VLOOKUP.

INDEX gives you the value of a cell based on its position in the spreadsheet.

How many planes were sold in February? In this example, your goal is cell C4, this cell is in row 4 and column C. The syntax is the following: INDEX(row, column), like if you were playing Battleship. To find the X and Y coordinates you can use two MATCH functions nested within the INDEX function.

Formula in D7 =INDEX(B2:D5,MATCH("Planes",A2:A5,0),MATCH("February",B1:D1,0))

	A	B	C	D
1		January	February	March
2	Cars	3	7	2
3	Trucks	5	1	4
4	Planes	2	3	4
5	Boats	6	4	5
6				
7				3

The equivalent formula using SUMPRODUCT would be:

SUMPRODUCT(B2:D5*(B1:D1="February")*(A2:A5="Planes"))

IF – This function is the typical logical IF → THEN statement, and it can be especially useful and save you time.

The function has 3 parts: IF(logical test, if the logical test is true then…, if not then…)

If the temperature of these cities is below freezing, type "Yes". The function you would need to use in cell C2 is =IF(B2<32,"Yes","No"). Anytime you face an if-then situation think about this function.

	A	B	C
1		Temperature (F)	Below Freezing?
2	New York	30	Yes
3	Miami	90	No
4	Raleigh	70	No
5	Chicago	15	Yes

Check tip #7 for nested IF functions.

OFFSET – This function returns a cell that is a specified number of rows and columns from another cell.

In your finance trend, which month is the latest month of actuals? The function you could use is a combination of OFFSET, INDEX, and COUNTIF: =OFFSET(INDEX(B2:F2,1,COUNTIF(B2:F2,"Actual")),-1,0). The part of the function highlighted in yellow belongs to the OFFSET function. Once you find the location of the most recent "Actual" (cell D2 below) using the INDEX and COUNTIF functions, the OFFSET function moves that cell's reference one place up (-1), and (0) places laterally so you end up in cell D1, which responds to the question. IMPORTANT: this function helps you automate your graphs and charts to show data from the latest month of actuals (or something equivalent) without having to update the range of your charts manually every week/month/year.

OFFSET(cell reference, rows, columns). Positive numbers in rows move your reference down, while negative numbers move it up; positive numbers in columns move your reference to the right, and negative numbers to the left.

	A	B	C	D	E	F
1		January	February	March	April	May
2		Actual	Actual	Actual	Forecast	Forecast
3	Sales	$ 50,000	$ 65,000	$ 90,000	$ 43,000	$ 33,000
4	Expenses	$ (15,000)	$ (24,000)	$ (40,000)	$ (20,000)	$ (10,000)
5	Profit	$ 35,000	$ 41,000	$ 50,000	$ 23,000	$ 23,000
6						
7						March

SUM & **AVERAGE** – Two of the easiest and simplest functions in Excel. They work well to add values and calculate averages.

- **Calculate Total Sales**: =SUM(B2:F2)

- **Calculate Monthly Average Sales**: =AVERAGE(B2:F2)

	A	B	C	D	E	F
1		January	February	March	April	May
2	Sales	$ 1,000	$ 500	$ 700	$ 1,200	$ 200
3						
4				Total		$ 3,600
5				Monthly Average		$ 720

2. **EXCEL FUNCTIONS FOR THE OTHER 5% OF THE TIME**

MONTH – This function returns the number of the month of a date, so it will vary between 1 and 12.

> You can use this for look up purposes if you are given a timeline and need to find data within one month. Use the following function in cell B1 (and through E1): =MONTH(B2). Another trick I used in cell G1 to go from just month name to month number is =MONTH(1&G2) = 3.

	A	B	C	D	E	F	G
1	Month?	1	3	5	7		3
2	Date	1/7/2022	3/4/2022	5/20/2022	7/13/2022		March

YEAR – This is equivalent to the function above, giving you the year instead.

> Use the following function in cell B1 (and through E1): =YEAR(B2)

	A	B	C	D	E
1	Year?	2020	2021	2022	2023
2	Date	1/7/2020	3/4/2021	5/20/2022	7/13/2023

MID – This function returns as many characters as you want from a given text.

> **Extract the number of kids Julia has in the example**. The function to use is =MID(A1,11,1). This means that you count "11" characters (spaces included) and once you reach the character you want, you choose how many more characters you want. In this case we only want the number of kids, so we choose "1" since "2" is only one character.

	A	B	C
1	Julia has 2 kids		2

LEN – Do you want to know how many characters there are in a given text? This formula tells you its LENgth.

	A	B	C
1	Julia has 2 kids		16

=LEN(A1)

AND – This logical function helps you group conditions to see if they **all** are true or not.

What bonus will our sales representatives receive? The function to use in E2 is =IF(AND(B2>=B5,C2>=B6),D2*5%,0%). Read this function like "if our sales representatives bring in 6 clients or more (B2>=B5) **and** if their sales are $40,000 or higher (C2>=B6), then their bonus is 5% of their commission; If they don't meet <u>both</u> conditions, their bonus is zero."

	A	B	C	D	E
1		Clients	Sales	Commission (15%)	Bonus (5%)
2	Jessica	5	$60,000	$9,000	$0
3	Mark	7	$45,000	$6,750	$338
4					
5	Clients goal	6			
6	Sales goal	$40,000			

OR – This logical function shows TRUE if at least one of the conditions is true.

What bonus will our sales representatives receive? The function to use in E2 is =IF(OR(B2>=B5,C2>=B6),D2*5%,0%). You can read this function like "if our sales representatives bring in 6 clients or more (B2>=B5), **or** if their sales are $40,000 or higher (C2>=B6), then their bonus is 5% of their commission". If they meet <u>at least 1</u> of the 2 conditions, they get a 5% bonus; if they don't meet any condition, their bonus is zero.

	A	B	C	D	E
1		Clients	Sales	Commission (15%)	Bonus (5%)
2	Jessica	5	$60,000	$9,000	$450
3	Mark	7	$45,000	$6,750	$338
4					
5	Clients goal	6			
6	Sales goal	$40,000			

COLUMN – This function tells you the position or number of a column.

For example, if you need the position or number for column "BT" you enter =COLUMN(BT1) , which equals 72.

If you type =COLUMN() leaving the reference empty, then you get the number of the column where your function is located.

ROW – This function tells you the position or number of a row.

Rows are embedded in cell references (i.e., A5) so you know already that it is referencing row 5. However, it will not be so easy in other instances, so if you need to know the row number then this function would become useful.

If you type =ROW() leaving the reference empty, then you get the number of the row where your function is located.

CONCATENATE – This function helps you join text strings into just one text string.

How do you combine our customers' first and last names? The formula you use in C2 is =CONCATENATE(A2," ",B2). Note the expression " " in between the first and last name. This adds a space between the first and last name. CONCATENATE is Excel's built-in solution for this, but you could also do it without the CONCATENATE function using the character "&", like this: =A2&" "&B2

	A	B	C
1	First name	Last name	Full name
2	Jack	Ryan	Jack Ryan
3	Kobe	Bryant	Kobe Bryant

COUNT – This function counts numbers stored as values, ignoring empty cells and numbers stored as text. =COUNT(B2:E2)

Note how N/A in March does not get counted

	A	B	C	D	E	F	G
1		January	February	March	April		COUNT
2	Sales	$500	$340	N/A	$560		3

COUNTA – This function counts all cells within a range as long as they are not empty. =COUNTA(B2:E2)

Note how N/A in March does get counted

	A	B	C	D	E	F	G
1		January	February	March	April		COUNTA
2	Sales	$500	$340	N/A	$560		4

EOMONTH – This function returns the last day of the month **n** months before or after a given date.

This function is useful to set deadlines. The function you insert in cell C2 is =EOMONTH(A2,B2)

Check tip #11 to learn how to show the first and the last day of a month using this function.

	A	B	C
1	Date	Month	EOMONTH
2	3/7/2021	1	4/30/2021
3	2/4/2022	3	5/31/2022
4	5/2/2022	-2	3/31/2022

ROUND – This function rounds a number to as many decimals you choose.

Round these students' GPA to the second decimal place. The function you need in cell C2 is =ROUND(B2,2). First you select the number you want to round (B2), then enter the number of decimals you want to round to (2).

	A	B	C
1		GPA	Rounded GPA
2	Christy	3.43501	3.44
3	Robert	3.79639	3.80
4	William	3.92383	3.92

LEFT – This function extracts as many text characters as you want starting at the **beginning** of the text string.

	A	B
1	Michael Jordan is the GOAT	
2		Michael Jordan

=LEFT(A1,14). 14 is the number of characters in "Michael Jordan".

RIGHT – This function extracts as many text characters as you want starting at the **end** of the text string.

	A	B
1	Michael Jordan is the GOAT	
2		GOAT

=RIGHT(A1,4). 4 is the number of characters in "GOAT".

VALUE – This function changes numbers stored as text into actual numbers you can work with.

Extract the number of cars sold every month and add them up. The problem here is that when you extract numbers from a text string, those numbers are stored as text, so your SUM(C2:C4) function will not work correctly in cell C6 when adding those numbers up (see how cell C6 shows 0). You must store them as VALUES first, and only then you can work with them. Note the difference between the following two functions.

In cell C2 (number stored as text): =LEFT(B2,LEN(B2)-15)

In cell D2 (number stored as value): =VALUE(LEFT(B2,LEN(B2)-15))

Function in D2 extracts the number of cars sold and converts it to values. It starts by looking at the LENgth of cell B2, then it subtracts 15 characters to that length because " cars were sold" = 15 characters. By doing this you remove all characters from the text string in B2 except for the actual characters you are interested in ("50"), which then you turn into values. No matter if 1,000 cars were sold, that function in D2 will work every time so you do not have to tweak it.

	A	B	C	D
1		Sales	Number as text	Number as value
2	January	50 cars were sold	50	50
3	February	46 cars were sold	46	46
4	March	62 cars were sold	62	62
5				
6		Total	0	158

VLOOKUP – Many companies include in their job postings that you need to know how to use VLOOKUP.

It is key to learn how to use this formula to look up information in tables. That said, INDEX-MATCH-MATCH and SUMPRODUCT are better because they are applicable to more scenarios.

The table below shows three sales representatives from CarMax and their best-selling cars each month. **Which car brand did Mike sell the most in February?** The function you need in D6 is =VLOOKUP("Mike",A1:D4,3,FALSE). "V" in VLOOKUP stands for Vertical so think about this as a function that scans a chosen column from top to bottom to find the information. First you choose which value you want to find in the very first column ("Mike"), then you select the entire range of the table (A1:D4), and then enter the number of the column in which you want to look up (February is column number 3 within the range A1:D4). It is not mandatory for the function to work, but I recommend finishing entering the word "FALSE" (or a "0") to make sure the function finds exactly "Mike" in the first column and not something just approximately similar.

	A	B	C	D
1		January	February	March
2	**Charles**	Ford	Dodge	Tesla
3	**Mike**	Chrysler	Ford	Honda
4	**Ashley**	Toyota	BMW	Honda
5				
6			VLOOKUP	Ford

HLOOKUP – Because of how data is typically structured in tables, HLOOKUP is not as commonly used as VLOOKUP. "H" in HLOOKUP stands for Horizontal so think about this as a function that scans a chosen row from left to right to find the information. **What was the lowest temperature in Madrid in 2021?**
=HLOOKUP("Madrid",B1:E4,3,FALSE)

	A	B	C	D	E	F	G	H
1		Sydney	Madrid	Tokyo	Denver			
2	Highest temperature in 2021	94	117	81	73		HLOOKUP	3
3	Lowest temperature in 2021	43	3	27	-1			
4	Average temperature in 2021	55	65	62	48			

IFERROR – This function helps you handle errors such as #VALUE! and instead shows the custom result you choose.

> **Extract Ross', Lilly's and Ronald's GPAs from the table and calculate their average.** Function in E1 is =VLOOKUP(D1,A1:B5,2,0) but it shows an error when looking for "Ross'" GPA because he isn't in the student list. Therefore, the =AVERAGE(E1:E3) function in E5 shows an error as well. Fix this by adding an IFERROR function that encapsules your original VLOOKUP function. The function in I1 is =IFERROR(VLOOKUP(D1,D1:E5,2,0),"Not Found"). Now, whenever the encapsuled function (VLOOKUP) shows an error, the output will be "Not Found". Also, because AVERAGE is a function that ignores text ("Not Found" in I1), now the formula in I5 works correctly.

	A	B	C	D	E	F	G	H	I
1	**Student**	**GPA**		Ross	#N/A				Not Found
2	Josh	3.40		Lilly	3.8		→		3.8
3	Frank	3.70		Ronald	3.2				3.2
4	Lilly	3.80							
5	Ronald	3.20		Average	#N/A				3.5

ISNUMBER – You are not wrong if you assume that this function tells you whether the content of a cell is a number.

> **Create a form to check student GPAs. Search by Student ID. For confidentiality reasons, if you search by student name it must display an error.**
>
> The function in cell H3 is =IF(ISNUMBER(F3),VLOOKUP(F3,A2:C4,3,0),"Error. Use Student ID"). IF you enter a number in cell F3, then it will trigger the VLOOKUP function; if you do not enter a number, it will trigger the error. Remember that the power of Excel is in being able to combine multiple functions.

	A	B	C	D	E	F	G	H
1	**Student ID**	**Name**	**GPA**					
2	34920	Julia Smith	4.0					Result
3	55299	Thomas Paine	3.6		Search Box	34920	→	4.00
4	34610	Steve Rogers	3.7		Search Box	Julia Smith		Error. Use Student ID

MAX / MIN – These two functions return the highest and the lowest numbers from selected cells.

What car brand from the list is the most expensive? And the one with the lowest mileage?

The function in cell F2 is =INDEX(A2:A7,MATCH(MAX(B2:B7),B2:B7,0)). First, we find the largest price, then we use that as a reference in our INDEX-MATCH to find the associated car brand on column A.

The function in cell F2 is =INDEX(A2:A7,MATCH(MIN(C2:C7),C2:C7,0)). First, we find the lowest mileage, then we use that as a reference in our INDEX-MATCH to find the associated car brand on column A.

	A	B	C	D	E	F
1	Cars	Average Price	Mileage (mpg)			
2	Ferrari	$380,000	18		MAX price	Ferrari
3	Lincoln	$75,000	19		MIN mileage	Bentley
4	BMW	$65,000	25			
5	Ford	$43,000	23			
6	Toyota	$35,000	24			
7	Bentley	$270,000	17			

TRIM – **This function normalizes spacing in text strings.**

Sometimes you download data from a database, and it comes with leading spaces or multiple spaces between words, making your formulas show errors. TRIM eliminates leading spaces and leaves just one space between words, making it easy for you to work with your data. Function in cell E3 is =TRIM(A3)

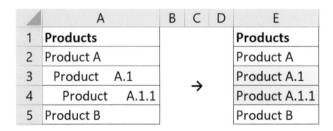

	A	B	C	D	E
1	Products				Products
2	Product A				Product A
3	Product A.1				Product A.1
4	Product A.1.1				Product A.1.1
5	Product B				Product B

NETWORKDAYS – This function calculates the number of working days between dates.

This formula only counts from Monday to Friday. Optionally you can include a list of holidays that the function would also exclude if they fell between Monday and Friday. If you want to exclude holidays, create another table for it first.

Function in C2 is =NETWORKDAYS(A2,B2)   Function in D2 is =NETWORKDAYS(A2,B2,F2:F8)

	A	B	C	D	E	F
1	Date A	Date B	Incl. holidays	Excl. holidays		Holidays
2	1/3/2021	9/12/2021	180	176		1/1/2021
3	4/6/2021	9/20/2021	120	119		1/18/2021
4	3/15/2021	7/25/2021	95	94		1/20/2021
5						2/15/2021
6						5/31/2021
7						6/19/2021
8						7/4/2021

SUBTOTAL – It creates subtotals, but the coolest functionality is that it allows you to sum numbers ignoring hidden rows.

Sometimes you filter rows to see different cuts, but your SUM function keeps showing you the total including filtered rows, so your SUM function is not useful. The solution for this is the function SUBTOTAL, and it works not only to SUM numbers but also for AVERAGEs, MIN/MAX, and more. The function in cell C9 is =SUBTOTAL(109,C2:C6). Note number '109', which makes SUBTOTAL sum ignoring filtered cells.

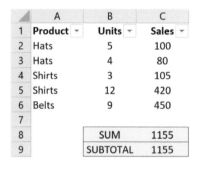

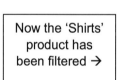

Now the 'Shirts' product has been filtered →

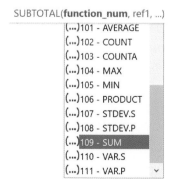

3. HOW TO COMBINE AND, AND OR FUNCTIONS

The ability to combine functions AND, and OR can save you time and effort when analyzing data. It can get complex, so when in doubt, write down all conditions separately and then start combining them. In this example, we want to know if there is any product in our portfolio with a sales margin higher than 20% that **also** meets **at least one** of three other conditions: it must be red, it must be made in Spain, or its price must be between $45 and $100.

The function we use in F2 is
=IF(AND(OR(D2="Spain",B2="Red",AND(C2>=45,C2<=100)),A2>20%),"Yes","No")

The last item's margin is higher than 20% and was made in Spain, so it meets the first condition and at least one of the other three mentioned.

	A	B	C	D	E	F
1	Margin	Color	Price	Country		Meets conditions?
2	15%	Green	$50	France		No
3	20%	Red	$30	Italy		No
4	35%	Yellow	$120	Spain		Yes

4. HOW TO DELETE BLANK ROWS

You are cleaning up a database and you want to delete every row where at least one of the fields is blank. Select all your data, then Home>Find & Select>Go to Special….>Select "Blanks" >OK. This selects all your blanks. Now Click on Delete>Delete Sheet Rows

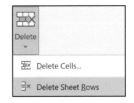

	A	B	C	D
1	ID	Item	Color	Cost
2	45G22D	Shoes		$43
3	U8FFRM	Hat	Green	$12
4		Sunglasses	Blue	
5		Watch	White	$90
6	23CMPU	Shirt	Red	$32
7	PSBN88		Black	$9

	A	B	C	D
1	ID	Item	Color	Cost
2	U8FFRM	Hat	Green	$12
3	23CMPU	Shirt	Red	$32

5. UNPROTECT A WORKSHEET OR WORKBOOK WITHOUT KNOWING THE PASSWORD?

Unprotecting a Worksheet

Hack your own file. You will need software that can open .zip files. Free options: WinZip, WinRaR or 7-Zip.

1. Close your spreadsheet and make a copy of the file just in case you break it.

2. In the explorer with the file extensions showing up, replace the ".xlsx" / ".xls" / ".xlsm" / ".xlsb" extension in the name by ".zip".

3. Double-click in the file to open it. Open the "xl" folder, then "worksheets" and you should see as many results as tabs you have in your workbook (i.e., "Sheet1.xml", "Sheet2.xml"…). Double-click on the sheet that was protected.

4. Press Ctrl+F and look up the work "protection". You should be directed to a piece of code that looks like this:

```
<sheetProtection algorithmName="SHA-
512" hashValue="QZlcpETYSGbT/+W1JKpIePhmDpRKUFgnNTszwQdtysEiRsnBX6/zaGtEcfyLfFqz
iKYrULfd7aiTCYv0Nv+ZWw==" saltValue="XDgjMXIPu+Coh7L91aNDEQ==" spinCount="100000
" sheet="1" objects="1" scenarios="1"/>
```

5. After confirming that you see that piece of code in the sheet you opened, make a copy of this sheet file somewhere else (i.e., your Desktop). Now we want to edit this copy, so right click/Open with/Notepad.

6. Press Ctrl+F and look for "protection". Select the entire piece of code you see above including the two brackets (< >) and delete it. Be careful. If you don't delete exactly this, you might break it. Then, save and close the file.

7. Copy the file you just saved and paste it in the .zip folder. If your sheet was called "sheet2.xml", paste the new one that you have just updated, and it will replace the old one with the same name. Paste and hit "OK".

8. Close the ".zip" file and change its extension back to its original one (".xlsx" or others, depending on your case). Congratulations, you have hacked your worksheet to remove its protection!

Unprotecting a Workbook *(not valid for password-encrypted workbooks. That requires brute force and special software)*.

Follow steps 1 and 2 above. Double-click in the file to open it. Click on "xl" and then you should see a file called "workbook.xml". Double-click on the file to open it. Continue with steps 4 through 8 above.

6. CONDITIONAL FORMATTING OF CELLS

Sometimes we can get lost in the data when there are too many numbers and maybe we overlook something that is important. Excel offers preset conditional formatting, but we have the option of creating our own rules using logical functions.

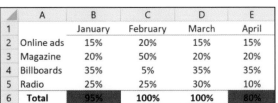

Click on "Conditional Formatting", and then on "New Rule". In the first example below, check if our marketing budget is 100% allocated every month; In the second example, highlight names that do not coincide in columns A and B.

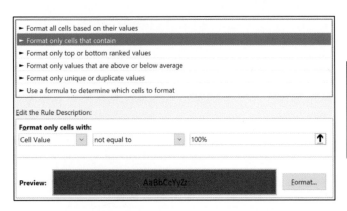

	A	B	C	D	E
1		January	February	March	April
2	Online ads	15%	20%	15%	15%
3	Magazine	20%	50%	20%	20%
4	Billboards	35%	5%	35%	35%
5	Radio	25%	25%	30%	10%
6	**Total**	95%	100%	100%	80%

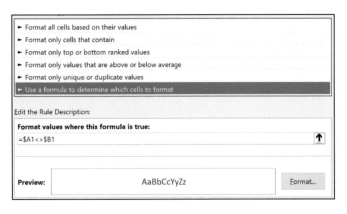

	A	B
1	Microsoft	Microsoft
2	Apple	Apple Inc
3	JCPenney	JC Penney
4	Wal-Mart	Walmart
5	Tesla Inc	Tesla Inc

7. HOW TO CREATE A NESTED IF FUNCTION

A nested IF function is multiple IF functions combined. **How would you assign grades to these students based on their test scores?** Below, I used three nested IF functions in C2: =IF(B2<65,"D",IF(B2<80,"C",IF(B2<91,"B","A")))

The false part of the IF statement becomes a new IF function.

IF(logical_test, value_if_true, IF(logical_test, value_if_true, IF(logical_test, value_if_true, value_if_false)))

	A	B	C	D	E	F
1	Student	Score	Grade		Score	Grade
2	Mark	75	C		91-100	A
3	Rob	92	A		80-90	B
4	Jessica	86	B		65-79	C
5	Tracy	55	D		<65	D

8. HOW TO DRAG A FORMULA TO SAVE TIME

You drag a formula up, down, left or right to copy an existing formula into adjacent cells that will use the same formula. This saves you time by not having to re-type functions. The world divides between those who use the keyboard for everything, and those who use the mouse. Remember that copying formulas and locking references (see tip #24) go always hand in hand.

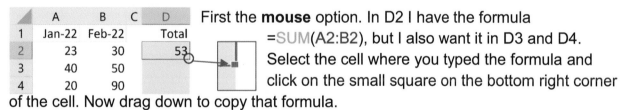

First the **mouse** option. In D2 I have the formula =SUM(A2:B2), but I also want it in D3 and D4. Select the cell where you typed the formula and click on the small square on the bottom right corner of the cell. Now drag down to copy that formula.

If you use your **keyboard** for this example, select cell D2 and copy it (Ctrl+C). Then press Shift and use the arrows on the keyboard to highlight the range where you want that formula copied. Once you have highlighted the entire range, press Ctrl+D. If you were copying horizontally to the right, press Ctrl+R instead.

You can also enter formulas using your keyboard. For example, click on cell D2 and, in this order, do:

Type "=SUM", hit the "tab" key (it adds the parenthesis), press the left arrow (←) twice (to go to B2), now press Shift and hit the left arrow (←) once. Hit Enter to finish.

9. HOW TO REFERENCE EXCEL TABLES

By Excel table here I mean the ones you create pressing Ctrl+T. Those tables that have their own name, banded rows that help differentiate the data, and filters at the top row (the header).

You might have noticed that the formulas look different when you reference one of these tables, like here:

Not an Excel table

D6 = MAX(B2:C4)

"Range" reference

	A	B	C	D
1	Item	January	February	
2	Cars	7	5	
3	Trucks	2	6	
4	Vans	4	4	
5				
6	Largest number sold of any item in a month			7

An Excel table

D6 = MAX(Sales[[January]:[February]])

"Structured" reference.

	A	B	C	D
1	Item	January	February	
2	Cars	7	5	
3	Trucks	2	6	
4	Vans	4	4	
5				
6	Largest number sold of any item in a month			7

It references all values from the January and February columns of the table called "Sales". And the double bracket ([[and]]) is equivalent to adding "$" to both the column and row of a range reference. You would remove just one set of brackets to remove this absolute reference. However, what if next month you have an additional month (March)? That function would not work anymore because you would not capture March's data. The best way to fix this to make sure you always reference the complete set of values regardless of the headers of the table. To do this, use the reference "#Data" like in =MAX(Sales[#Data]).

Also, if you use the reference [[January]:[February]] for lookup functions such as Index Match, it's recommended to use [#Headers] instead. This way you will always reference all headers, not just two (unless you just want those two).

10. HOW TO SHOW A NUMBER IN THOUSANDS, MILLIONS, BILLIONS...

Select the number whose format you are interested in changing and hit "Ctrl+1" to open the Cell Format options. Below you see different options. Each coma (,) you type divides the number by 1,000. Add "K", "MM", or "B" if you want to show more details beside the number itself.

	A	B	C
1		Number	Cell Format
2	Whole $	1,000,000,000	#,##0.00
3	Millions	1,000	#,##0,,
4	Billions	1	#,##0,,,
5	(MM)	1,000 MM	#,##0,, "MM"
6	(B)	1 B	#,##0,, "B"

11. SHOW ME THE LAST DAY OF THE MONTH

There is a function that gives you the last day of the month for a given date, and you can also use it to obtain the first day of the month.

Formula in C2: =EOMONTH(A2,0)

Formula in D2: =EOMONTH(A2,-1)+1

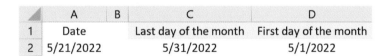

	A	B	C	D
1	Date		Last day of the month	First day of the month
2	5/21/2022		5/31/2022	5/1/2022

12. HOW DOES SOLVER WORK? SOLVING A MAGIC SQUARE

Solver is a hidden gem. It is an Excel add-in that helps you find solutions for systems of equations. Additionally, it can find the optimal solution when there are possible valid ones, like if you had to spend a budget in an efficient way.

As an example, let's solve a magic square. A magic square is a mathematical challenge where you must find the numbers that match certain criteria. It requires the sum of each row, column, and diagonal to be equal. The problem statement would be: **_Using integers from 1 to 9, find a combination where every row, column, and diagonal sum 15._**

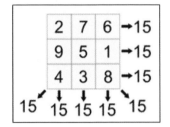

First, build the 3x3 template and enter SUM formulas in the grey cells, where you want to see the sum of every row, column, and diagonal.

Next, open Solver and add conditions to find the result you are looking for:
- Set Objective: We do not need a solution only in one specific cell, so you can leave it empty
- Variable cells: These are the cells Solver will populate with numbers from 1 to 9
- Constraints:
  - AllDifferent – all the Variable cells must be different
  - Integer – all the Variable cells must be integers
  - The sum of values in each column, row and diagonal must equal 15

13. EXTRACT TEXT BEFORE OF AFTER SPACE

	A	B	C	D	E
1	Name		Extract...	Result	Formula
2	Javier S. Sanz		Before 1st space	Javier	=LEFT(A2,(FIND(" ",A2,1)-1))
3			After 1st space	S. Sanz	=MID(A2,FIND(" ",A2)+1,LEN(A2))
4			Before 2nd space	Javier S.	=LEFT(A2,SEARCH(" ",A2,SEARCH(" ",A2)+1))
5			After 2nd space	Sanz	=RIGHT(A2,LEN(A2)-(SEARCH(" ",A2,SEARCH(" ",A2)+1)))
6			Between 2 spaces	S.	=MID(A2,FIND(" ",A2)+1,FIND(" ",A2,FIND(" ",A2)+1)-FIND(" ",A2))

Change " " for a comma "," if your words are delimited by a comma. Also remember the functionality from tip #35

14. HOW TO COLOR CELLS BASED ON A CONDITION

Select the data you want to apply colors to, then click on Conditional Formatting and choose the condition. Below I am coloring months where sales where higher than $50,000.

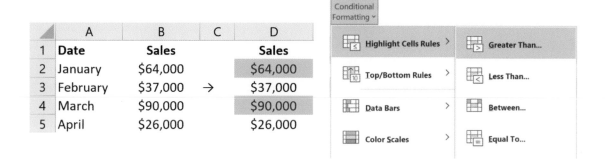

15. HOW TO COUNT COLORED CELLS

There are multiple ways to count colored cells. Easy and quick ones, and other ones more complex that include programming VBA code. The thing is that cells are colored normally for a reason (a condition), so what I recommend for counting colored cells is to use the function COUNTIF. In the example above you could use function =COUNTIF(B2:B5,">50000") which is equivalent to literally counting colored cells. Another quick solution is to use =SUBTOTAL(102,B2:B5) and then filter by color to count those cells.

16. HOW CAN EXCEL FILL IN THE BLANKS ON A WORD DOCUMENT?

This solution is useful for lawyers who use templates for contracts where the same word appears frequently.

We will start by creating the below table in Excel with all the unique fields we want to replace in the Word document.

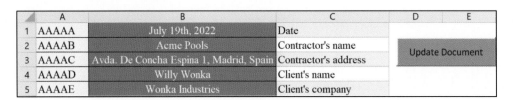

	A	B	C	D	E
1	AAAAA	July 19th, 2022	Date		
2	AAAAB	Acme Pools	Contractor's name		
3	AAAAC	Avda. De Concha Espina 1, Madrid, Spain	Contractor's address	Update Document	
4	AAAAD	Willy Wonka	Client's name		
5	AAAAE	Wonka Industries	Client's company		

Excel will search the codes from column A in the Word document, and every time it identifies one, it will replace the code with the assigned text from column B. This means you type each field just once, while Excel will replace it as many times as it appears in Word, reducing time and the risk for typos. We will write the code below for this.

```
Private Sub CommandButton1_Click()
Dim ws As Worksheet, msWord As Object, itm As Range
    Set ws = ActiveSheet
    Set msWord = CreateObject("Word.Application")
    With msWord
        .Visible = True
        .Documents.Open "C:\Users\javier\Desktop\Contract1.docx"
        .Activate

    With .ActiveDocument.Content.Find
        .ClearFormatting
        .Replacement.ClearFormatting

        For Each itm In ws.UsedRange.Columns("A").Cells
            .Text = itm.Value2 'Look for the codes from column A
            .Replacement.Text = itm.Offset(, 1).Value2  'Replace with what's in column B
            .MatchCase = False
            .MatchWholeWord = False
            .Execute Replace:=2
        Next
    End With

    End With

End Sub
```

Before and After in the Word document after executing the macro:

This CONSTRUCTION WORK CONTRACT ("Contract"), dated AAAAA ("Effective Date"), is entered by and between AAAAB ("Contractor") at AAAAC and AAAAD of AAAAE ("Client").

This CONSTRUCTION WORK CONTRACT ("Contract"), dated JULY 19TH, 2022 ("Effective Date"), is entered by and between ACME POOLS ("Contractor") at AVDA. DE CONCHA ESPINA 1, MADRID, SPAIN and WILLY WONKA of WONKA INDUSTRIES ("Client").

17. SHORTCUTS TO BECOME SUPER-EFFICIENT

The same way you want a high-speed Internet connection to watch Tiger King in 4K on Netflix, you will want to have a quick-access ribbon to work fast with Excel. Mine has 95% of the functions I use in Excel, so I do not have to go through the normal ribbons.

1. **Save** – You can also press Ctrl+S, but if it is in the ribbon that makes it one less shortcut to remember.

2. **Undo** – If your work is about trial and error, you will click here often. You can also do Ctrl-Z to undo.

3. **Redo** – Maybe you were right and want to redo what you just undid? Click here or press Ctrl+Y.

4. **Filter** – Is it worth remembering the shortcut Ctrl+Shift+L to create filters? No, just click on it in one tenth of a second.

5. **Format Painter** – Hands down one of the best functionalities of Excel to save time when making your spreadsheet more visual. Double-click on it to apply the format to different sections without having to click on it multiple times. You can create your own custom shortcut for this, but again it is not worth it because it is one click away.

6. **Insert Columns** – Every now and then you need to insert columns between two pieces of existing information. Click here to add one column.

7. **Insert Rows** – Same as #6, but for rows.

8. **Insert Pivot Table** – Excel purists will look down on you because they use the shortcut Alt+V+N. This is one click.

9. **Trace Dependents** – This is your breadcrumb trail. It helps you understand how the spreadsheet works, especially when you inherited it from someone else. If you wonder if that cell has effects on another one, click here.

10. **Remove All Arrows** - #9 might display blue arrows all over your spreadsheet. This helps you remove them.

11. **Evaluate Formula** – Have you ever wondered how a formula gets calculated step by step? Click here to see how.

Those are the shortcuts that work for me, but you might want to add or remove some of them depending on your needs. The most important part is that you keep a quick-access ribbon.

Every time you add a shortcut to the quick-access ribbon, Excel creates an internal keyboard shortcut for it. Simply press the "Alt" key + the number that Excel associates to each of them to use it (i.e., Alt+5 for Format Painter).

SUPER-USEFUL KEYBOARD SHORTCUTS

- Ctrl+C / Ctrl+V – Copy/Paste also works in Excel to copy and paste formulas.

- Ctrl+[– This takes you to the source of the formula you clicked on to see where it comes from. Very good to navigate.

- Ctrl+1 – This is a quicker way to format cells.

- F2 – Press to edit a cell. It is an excellent way to identify what cells your functions are referencing.

- F4 – One of the best shortcuts. It works to lock references in your formulas instead of manually typing "$". Keep pressing it to use different combinations of it depending on what you need in each situation.

- F9 – Select a piece of a formula and press F9 to see the result of that specific calculation. Useful for long formulas.

- Ctrl+↓ / Ctrl+↑ / Ctrl+→ / Ctrl+← – navigate quickly to the next cell down/up/right/left.

- Ctrl+B / Ctrl + I / Ctrl+U – Like in Microsoft Word or PowerPoint, use this to **bold**, *italicize* and <u>underline</u> data.

- Ctrl+F / Ctrl+H – F to Find, H to replace. Especially the latter will save you time. You can use it in formulas too.

- Alt+Enter – Adds a line break inside of a cell. Useful to split long formulas in different rows so it's easier to read.

- Ctrl+D / Ctrl+R – It copies a formula down (D) or to the right (R). Press Shift to select multiple cells.

18. PIVOT TABLES ARE THE BREAD AND BUTTER OF EXCEL, HERE IS WHY

Pivot tables are the best way to summarize data in Excel and can be incredibly powerful at giving you the solutions you need when analyzing data.

Companies even specify in their job posts that you must be proficient working with Pivot Tables. In the example below (downloaded from *https://contextures.com*) you see the sales of a company.

	A	B	C	D	E	F	G
1	Data	Region	Rep	Item	Units	UnitCost	Total
2	1/7/2020	East	Jones	Pencil	95	1.99	189.05
3	2/8/2020	Central	Kivell	Binder	50	19.99	999.5
4	2/9/2020	Central	Jardine	Pencil	36	4.99	179.64
5	2/26/2020	Central	Gill	Pen	27	19.99	539.73
6	3/15/2020	West	Sorvino	Pencil	56	2.99	167.44
7	4/1/2020	East	Jones	Binder	60	4.99	299.4
8	4/18/2020	Central	Andrews	Pencil	75	1.99	149.25
9	5/5/2020	Central	Jardine	Pencil	90	4.99	449.1
10	5/22/2020	West	Thompson	Pencil	32	1.99	63.68
11	6/8/2020	East	Jones	Binder	60	8.99	539.4
12	6/25/2020	Central	Morgan	Pencil	90	4.99	449.1

For each sale (each row) you have different data: date, region, rep, item, units, unitcost, and total. **If your manager asks you how much each rep from each region sold each month**, how would you do it if the spreadsheet has tenths of thousands of rows? The best solution is a pivot table. Once you learn how to use them, you could finish this task in less than a minute.

First, select the data and create a pivot table (Insert > PivotTable) in a new worksheet.

	A	B	C	D	E	F	G	H
2		Jan	Feb	Mar	Apr	May	Jun	Grand Total
4	**Central**		$1,719		$149	$449	$449	$2,766
5	Andrews				$149			$149
6	Gill		$540					$540
7	Jardine		$180			$449		$629
8	Kivell		$1,000					$1,000
9	Morgan						$449	$449
10	**East**	$189			$299		$539	$1,028
11	Jones	$189			$299		$539	$1,028
12	**West**			$167		$64		$231
13	Sorvino			$167				$167
14	Thompson					$64		$64
15	**Grand Total**	$189	$1,719	$167	$449	$513	$989	$4,025

Now it is just about placing the fields of the table in the right spots, and the information you are looking for simply shows up. **Keep practicing different combinations until you get used to how it works!**

19. CAN EXCEL SEND EMAILS?

Short answer: yes.

Long answer: I'll show you how to create a button like this one  to send emails automatically via Outlook. When you click on it, whatever section you want from your spreadsheet will be pasted into a new spreadsheet, which then will get attached into a new email with a pre-populated subject, recipients, and body. This will save you some precious time if you must send Excel reports every day/week/month. This is technically coding, but you don't even need to know how to code. Follow the steps and it will work :)

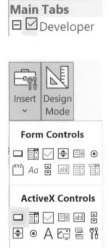

To create the button, you first need the "Developer" ribbon. Go to File/Options/Customize Ribbon and check the box for "Developer". A new ribbon will be added. Then click on Developer/Insert and click on "Command Button". Using the mouse, click anywhere and drag to create the button. To change its name, right click on it, select "CommandButton Object" and then "Edit". Name the button the way you want.

Let's go with the magic now. Right click on the button and select "View Code". You should see something like this:

```
Private Sub CommandButton1_Click()

End Sub
```

Now go to the next two pages and simply copy the content as is between the "Private Sub" and "End Sub" lines. Make sure your button's internal name is "CommandButton1". Otherwise, it won't work. You can check its internal name by right-clicking on the button you just created and then on "Properties". You can of course choose a different name, but you would also need to change it in the code.

Within the code, see in orange the code snippets that will allow you to adapt the code to your specific needs. I also added extra comments in green so that you know what the code is doing. Make sure the "Design Mode" button is turned off, otherwise you will not be able to click on the button you created.

```vba
Dim Source As Range
Dim Dest As Workbook
Dim wb As Workbook
Dim TempFilePath As String
Dim TempFileName As String
Dim FileExtStr As String
Dim FileFormatNum As Long
Dim OutApp As Object
Dim OutMail As Object
Dim signature As String

Set Source = Nothing
On Error Resume Next
Set Source = Range("A4:C13").SpecialCells(xlCellTypeVisible) 'This is the range of your
spreadsheet that you want to send by email. It will be copied and then pasted as values
into a new spreadsheet keeping its format.
On Error GoTo 0
If Source Is Nothing Then
    MsgBox "The source is not a range or the sheet is protected, please correct and try
again.", vbOKOnly
    Exit Sub
End If
With Application
    .ScreenUpdating = False
    .EnableEvents = False
End With
Set wb = ActiveWorkbook
Set Dest = Workbooks.Add(xlWBATWorksheet)
Source.Copy
With Dest.Sheets(1)
    Application.DisplayAlerts = False
    .Cells(1).PasteSpecial Paste:=8
    .Cells(1).PasteSpecial Paste:=xlPasteValues 'To paste as values
    .Cells(1).PasteSpecial Paste:=xlPasteFormats 'To paste keeping format
    .Cells(1).PasteSpecial Paste:=xlPasteColumnWidths
    ActiveWindow.Zoom = 85
    ActiveWindow.DisplayGridlines = False
    Application.DisplayAlerts = True
    .Cells(1).Select
    Application.CutCopyMode = False
End With
TempFilePath = Environ$("temp") & "\"
```

```vba
TempFileName = "Month-end file" & " " & Format(Now, "mmm-dd-yyyy") 'Choose the
name for the attached file. It also adds today's date.
If Val(Application.Version) < 12 Then
    'You use Excel 97-2003
    FileExtStr = ".xls": FileFormatNum = -4143
Else
    'You use Excel 2007-2016
    FileExtStr = ".xlsx": FileFormatNum = 51
End If
Set OutApp = CreateObject("Outlook.Application")
Set OutMail = OutApp.CreateItem(0)
With Dest
    .SaveAs TempFilePath & TempFileName & FileExtStr, FileFormat:=FileFormatNum
    On Error Resume Next
    With OutMail
        .Display
    End With
    signature = OutMail.body 'This adds your signature to your email
    With OutMail
        .to = "abc1@xx.com;abc2@xx.com" 'Here type the email addresses of recipients
        .CC = "abc3@xx.com;abc4@xx.com" 'Here type the email addresses of recipients
as CC
        .BCC = ""
        .Subject = "Monthly financial metrics" 'Choose the subject for the email
        .HTMLBody = "<p style='font-family:calibri;font-size:11pt'>" & "John, please see
attached the monthly metrics." & "<br>" & "<br>" & "Please let me know if you have any
questions." & "</p>" & .HTMLBody 'This is the body of the email. In two different lines.
        .Attachments.Add Dest.FullName
    End With
    On Error GoTo 0
    .Close savechanges:=False
End With
Kill TempFilePath & TempFileName & FileExtStr
Set OutMail = Nothing
Set OutApp = Nothing
With Application
    .ScreenUpdating = True
    .EnableEvents = True
End With
```

20. CAN EXCEL GENERATE RANDOM NUMBERS?

Yes, if you ever needed to create a random series of numbers, you can use the function =RANDBETWEEN(X,Y) to create random numbers between two numbers, where "x" is the lower end of the range, and "y" is the higher end. Here in the example, I used the function =RANDBETWEEN(1,20) in cells A1 through A5.

	A
1	7
2	3
3	8
4	19
5	10

Bear in mind that this formula will recalculate and show new random numbers every time a calculation happens in the spreadsheet. If you have a long series, this can make your spreadsheet slower because everything must recalculate. If you are just interested in having a random series of numbers, copy the numbers and paste them as values so that they don't change anymore.

21. HOW TO FIND TEXT AND REPLACE IT (WORKS IN FORMULAS TOO)

One of the most useful shortcuts when you work with computers is Ctrl+F. It works to find words in Google Chrome, Word, or Excel. Imagine you must update the name of a product in Excel and that this product is repeated 1,000 times across the spreadsheet. How would you do it to avoid spending 3 hours doing it manually? The best way is "**Find and Replace**", and now it will take you just a few seconds to perform this task. Press Ctrl+H. In "Find what" enter the original name you want to change (Facebook); and in "Replace with", the new name (Meta). Then click on "Replace All". This will have an effect in the entire spreadsheet. If you need just certain cells updated, select all of them first and then hit Ctrl+H. Once you hit "Replace All" it will only affect the selected cells.

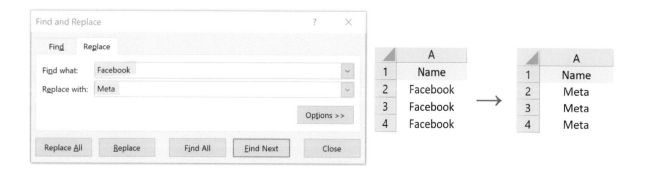

22. WHEN EXCEL SHOWS: #N/A, #REF!, #VALUE

It can be a little frustrating when you don't stop seeing errors in your functions, but once you understand why they show up, you will fix everything in the blink of an eye. If the function showing an error is a long one, **remember using** F9 for each section of the formula or the 🔘 "evaluate formula" shortcut to quickly identify which part of the function is causing the error.

#N/A → Your function can't find at least one of the references. Maybe you are asking a VLOOKUP to search for a name that doesn't exist in the first column of the range, or maybe the ranges you are using are not the right ones. Wrong names and ranges are the most typical reasons for #N/A errors, so check them first!

#REF! → This one can be a pain sometimes. It shows up when you reference a cell that no longer exists. The most typical case is when you remove rows or columns that were acting as inputs for a function. In the example below, I'm using the function =SUM(A1,A2,A3) in cell A5. If for whatever reason I remove row 2, the SUM formula will show a #REF! error because A2 has disappeared, and Excel doesn't know how to interpret this. It wouldn't show an error if my function were =SUM(A1:A3) so I recommend this format as much as possible.

	A
1	1
2	2
3	3
4	
5	6

#VALUE → This error happens when your function uses inputs in a format that cannot be used by that function. Imagine multiplying a number times a text string (i.e., 50 x "product"). There is no possible result for this, so Excel shows this error because at least one of the variables used is the wrong type. In this example you should multiply a number by another number.

23. WHEN EXCEL DOESN'T SCROLL

1. Most times the reason is that there are rows, columns or a combination of them frozen (check tip #25 on freezing panes). See on the right how to unfreeze panes.

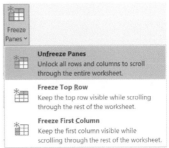

2. If the Shift key in your keyboard is pressed, Excel won't scroll. Check it isn't jammed.

3. Another reason, but also uncommon is that some keyboards have a Scroll Lock key, so make sure it is turned off.

24. HOW CAN I LOCK CELL REFERENCES IN EXCEL?

Locking cells is important because it saves you time and reduces the chances of making mistakes. If you are an experienced Excel user, you must have realized I haven't locked any references in my functions so far. I omitted them on purpose for the sake of simplicity, and because it makes the functions easier to read, thus easier to understand.

In Excel, we constantly drag formulas over or copy/paste functions in different cells to complete tasks. When we perform these actions, Excel replicates the format of the dragged/copied formula. For instance, if originally you were referencing A1 and then drag the function one place to the right, you will reference A2 in your new function. If you don't want this reference to change when dragging to the right, you must lock it by using the "$" symbol in the function → $A1.

The trick is knowing what to lock depending on your needs and you will know quickly after practicing. You can either lock rows (numbers), columns (letters), or both: A$2, $A2, $A$2. Within a formula, every time you type or select a reference you want to lock, I recommend you press F4. Press once and it will lock both rows and columns; press again and it will lock rows only; press one more time and it will lock columns only. Practice this and you will be much faster when working with Excel!

25. HOW CAN I FREEZE A ROW AND A COLUMN?

Click on "View" and then on Freeze Panes. This is especially useful to navigate through a large spreadsheet without losing your reference points. **Practice the following**: go to cell B4 and press Freeze Panes. Now try to scroll down and over to the right to experience what this function does for you. I highly recommend you using it if you have a long timeline with dates at the top. In the example below, all the green-shaded area gets fixed and won't move no matter if you scroll.

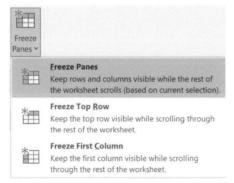

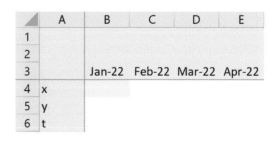

26. WHERE EXCEL SAVES TEMPORARY/BACKUP/AUTOSAVED FILES

I can't promise you will always recover unsaved files when Excel crashes, but here are a couple of tips to try to recover them.

1) In Excel go to File/Options/Save. Here you will find the location where Excel automatically saves AutoRecovered files. Now go check that location to see if a recent version of your file is there.

2) Open the Windows explorer, right click on your Excel file and then click on "Properties". The window below will show up. If there are old versions of your file that were saved automatically as backups, they will appear under "Previous Versions". Good luck!

27. WHICH EXCEL VERSION AM I USING?

- On Microsoft 365, click on File/Account and you will see your exact Excel version on the right-hand side.

- On Microsoft Office 2016, click on File/Account/About Excel. Then, find your Excel version at the top.

- On Microsoft Office 2010, click on File/Help, and you will see your exact version on the right side.

28. CAN I CREATE AN ALWAYS-VISIBLE DROPDOWN BUTTON?

Yes! If sending an email on tip #19 involved a long piece of code, this one can't be any shorter. **It's a nice little trick to let the users of your spreadsheet know that one cell is a dropdown.** Follow the steps below:

 Always visible!

1. Select one random cell and go to Insert/Symbol (on the very right) and click on "More Symbols". Change the font to *Wingdings 3* and select the highlighted character from the right. Then, click Insert. Change the color to grey and the font size to 8.

2. Using the Developer ribbon (see tip #19), click on "*Insert*" and select "*Command Button*", within **ActiveX Controls**. Click anywhere and drag to create the button. Now right click on it, Properties, and change its font to *Wingdings 3*.

3. Select the symbol you created on step #1 and copy it. Right click on the button you just created and select "*CommandButton Object*" and then "*Edit*". Now paste the symbol you had copied.

4. Right click on the button and select "*View code*". Once here, add the 2 lines of code highlighted in yellow from the right. Note that this code is referencing "C2" because my

```
Private Sub CommandButton1_Click()
Range("C2").Select
SendKeys "%{DOWN}"
End Sub
```

dropdown is in C2 as you can see above. Change this to match your dropdown's location. Also, make sure that your Command Button's name matches the one you see in the first line of the code (in my example, it's called "CommandButton1_Click", which is the name by default).

5. Close this window. **Now if you click on the button your dropdown list will be triggered!**

6. To finish, it will be a matter of formatting and placing the button in the right place so that it looks like a real button.

29. WHAT ARE CIRCULAR REFERENCES?

A circular reference in a cell is an error that happens when an Excel formula refers backs to the same cell where it is located. Because it is like a never-ending calculation, you will get the error message below. Imagine you enter the function =SUM(A1,A2) in A1. Because A1 is at the same time an input of the SUM function and the cell where the function is entered, this creates a circular reference.

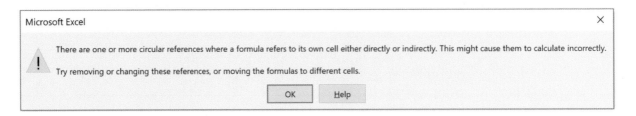

30. CAN I COMBINE TWO CELLS?

Yes, there are two ways:

1. Select all the cells you want to combine and click on the Merge & Center button ("Home" ribbon). It works to combine cells horizontally and vertically. If you are combining cells to show a long text, do not forget about the "Wrap Text" functionality to adjust your text to the size of your cell. *Tip: the more you can avoid merging cells, the better.*

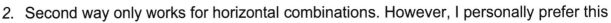

2. Second way only works for horizontal combinations. However, I personally prefer this way because merging cells like in the previous option might lead to errors when referencing cells to the combined cells. In general, try to avoid merging cells as much as you can. For this second option, select all the cells you want to combine and press Ctrl+1 to open the Format cells dialogue box. Then, click on Alignment. In the Horizontal dropdown box, select "Center Across Selection" and click on "OK".

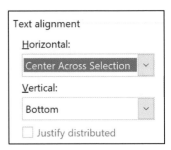

31. HOW TO SAVE EXCEL AS .PDF?

Click on File/Save As. Then, open the dropdown list (see below) and select "PDF (*.pdf)"

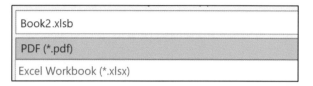

| Book2.xlsb |
| PDF (*.pdf) |
| Excel Workbook (*.xlsx) |

32. HOW CAN I PRINT MY ENTIRE SPREADSHEET ON ONE PAGE?

Ctrl+F is to Find what Ctrl+P is to Print. Once you go the print options, the option by default at the bottom is "No Scaling". With this option, our loan amortization schedule below would be printed in six pages. No bueno. Instead, select "**Fit Sheet on One Page**", and your entire sheet will be on just one page.

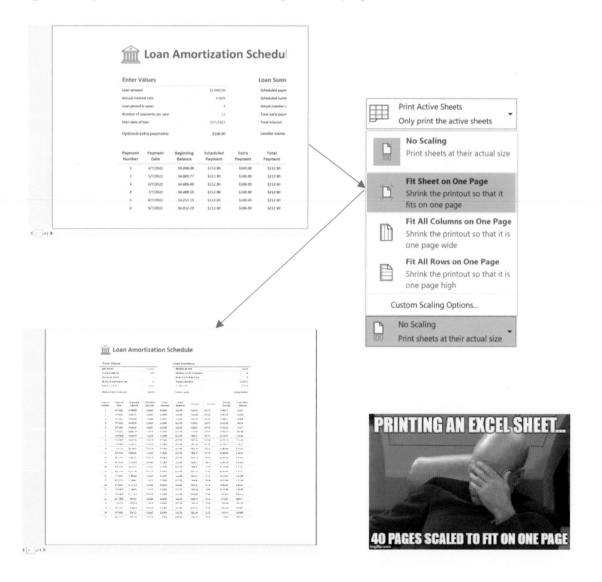

33. HOW TO CREATE GRAPHS WITH TWO AXES

Sometimes you have data that because of its size cannot be represented in just one axis because one of the items would not show up or because it would simply look weird. Two axes help us represent data that use different scales. If you insert a normal column chart using the data below, you get the first chart, where you cannot see data for Margin. The type of chart you want to create is called "Combo", and it allows you to choose whether one of the items goes to the secondary axis.

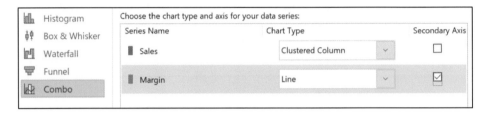

	January	February	March	April	May
Sales	50,000	65,000	70,000	45,000	55,000
Margin	20%	30%	25%	45%	30%

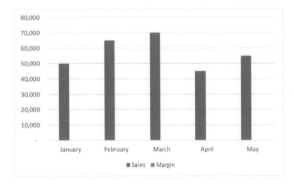
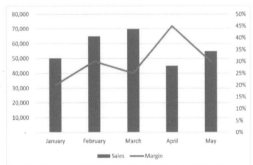

34. EXCEL WITHOUT GRIDLINES

If you create a spreadsheet that you or other people will often use, it helps if the design is clean. It always does. A great aid for this is removing the gridlines from the background. I would color the background white before discovering this option!

35. HOW TO SPLIT TEXT OR .CSV FILES INTO DIFFERENT COLUMNS

If you receive or download data where all the fields of a table are contained in just one column (like when using .CSV files - "Comma-Separated Values"), there is a quick way to separate each word into different columns. Select your data (A1:A4 in this case), go to the Data ribbon and click on the "Text to Columns" button. Next, in our case the option we must select is "Delimited", then Next. In the next screen, select how your data is delimited. In our case, it is delimited with a comma. Hit Next, and then Finish. Now each record is in a different column.

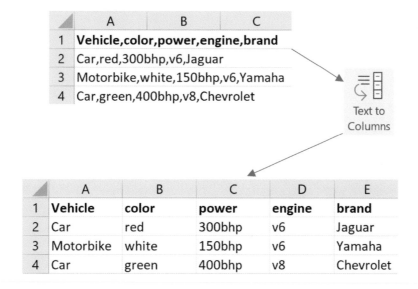

	A	B	C
1	Vehicle,color,power,engine,brand		
2	Car,red,300bhp,v6,Jaguar		
3	Motorbike,white,150bhp,v6,Yamaha		
4	Car,green,400bhp,v8,Chevrolet		

Text to Columns

	A	B	C	D	E
1	Vehicle	color	power	engine	brand
2	Car	red	300bhp	v6	Jaguar
3	Motorbike	white	150bhp	v6	Yamaha
4	Car	green	400bhp	v8	Chevrolet

36. HOW TO FIND AND DELETE DUPLICATES

You are organizing your Bitcoin addresses and, given how long they are, it is hard for you to spot duplicated addresses. How do you highlight those ones that are either unique or duplicated in your list? Home>Conditional Formatting>Highlight Cells Rules>Duplicate Values…>Select "Duplicate" and click OK.

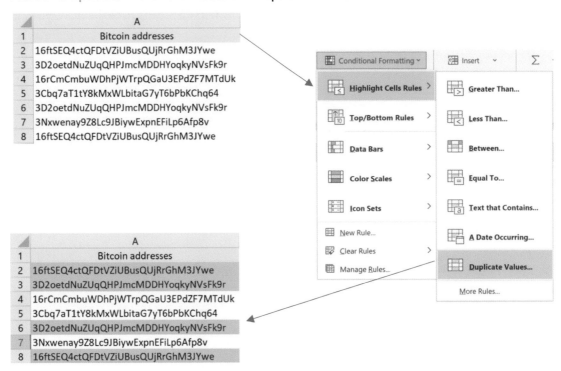

Even without highlighting duplicated values first, if you want to go ahead and remove any duplicates, select all data, then go to the Data ribbon and click on the "Remove Duplicates" button.

37. HOW TO CREATE CUSTOM FILTERS

You have an extensive list of products you want to sort by price from largest to smallest and, for those items that have the same price, you want them sorted by the number of items sold from largest to smallest. How do you filter the list using more than one condition? Home > Sort & Filter > Custom Sort. ⎸↑⎹ Custom Sort…
Now start adding conditions in the order you want, first Cost, and then Units, both sorted from largest to smallest. Click "Add Level" for additional conditions.

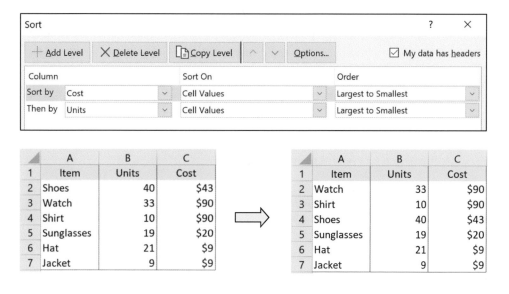

38. HOW TO CREATE DROP-DOWN LISTS

Drop-down lists are useful to select just one option out of a list in a clean way and without having to type anything. Go to Data> Data Validation ⎹ Data Validation > List . If you have just a few options for your list, you can type them out like in the first example below; otherwise, enter the range where all options are listed. Drop-down lists are very powerful when combined with logical functions such as IF, AND, OR, etc. This is because it allows you to create multiple scenarios, or change charts based on the value of the drop-down. Therefore, they are useful to create interactive dashboards.

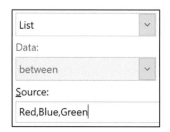

39. HOW TO EXTRACT TEXT FROM A STRING

There are multiple ways, the most used ones are LEFT, RIGHT, and MID.

LEFT will extract characters starting at the beginning of the string; RIGHT from the end; and MID from a given starting point.

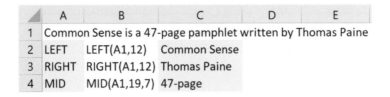

	A	B	C	D	E
1	Common Sense is a 47-page pamphlet written by Thomas Paine				
2	LEFT	LEFT(A1,12)	Common Sense		
3	RIGHT	RIGHT(A1,12)	Thomas Paine		
4	MID	MID(A1,19,7)	47-page		

40. WHAT IS THE ORDER OF MATH OPERATIONS IN EXCEL?

Excel uses the normal mathematical order: Parentheses > Exponents > Multiplication or Division > Addition or Subtraction. Excel calculates functions in this order, and for equivalent operations like multiplications and divisions, Excel will calculate from left to right. If you are in doubt, remember to use "Evaluate Formula": ![fx icon]

41. HOW TO CALCULATE DAYS BETWEEN TWO DATES

You have two options. Both are equally good.

a) Directly subtract both dates. As simple as =A2-A1 if you had your dates in those cells.

b) Use the DAYS function. =DAYS(end_date,start_date) → =DAYS(A2,A1)

42. WHEN TO USE THE FORMULA INT

The INT formula converts a number to the nearest integer rounding down. For example, if you are estimating the maximum number of units of something you can buy, use INT to remove decimals and stay conservative.

=INT(8.99) → returns 8

=INT(-8.99) → returns -9

43. HOW TO MOVE A CHART USING THE ARROWS ON THE KEYBOARD

Do you want to move your Excel chart in one direction using the keyboard arrows, but you are not able to do it? Press Ctrl + left mouse click. Now you can use the arrows to move charts. This is not needed in Excel 365.

44. COPY HORIZONTALLY, PASTE VERTICALLY OR VICE VERSA

It is called "transpose" and there are multiple ways to do it. Let's say you have 50 dates displayed horizontally, but you want them vertically. Doing it manually is not efficient so you can either:

a) Copy all dates and paste them selecting the "Transpose" option. See on the right →

b) Use the TRANSPOSE function. If you have your horizontal dates in A1:H1, use =TRANSPOSE(A1:H1) in A2 and Excel will show them vertically, but keeping the formula in all cells, so you might have to copy and paste them as values if you delete the original dates displayed horizontally.

45. CAN I BREAK AN EXCEL FORMULA INTO DIFFERENT LINES?

Long, complex or repetitive formulas might be hard to read, especially if you inherited them from somebody else. Make sure you make it easy for yourself and for others. Click on the formula where you want to break it, then hit "alt+Enter" to break the formula.

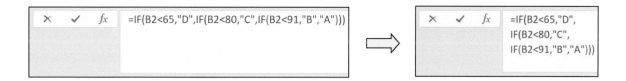

46. HOW TO HIGHLIGHT THE TOP 10 RESULTS

Select all your data, go to Home, click on Conditional Formatting and then on "Top/Bottom Rules", which are preset rules to highlight groups of results that meet a condition: top 10, bottom 10, above/below average…

47. HOW DO I PASSWORD PROTECT MY WORKBOOK?

Using a password, you can avoid that other user edits your workbook either totally or partially.

You can also select "Allow Edit Ranges" to specify which ranges other users can edit. This is helpful if you distribute templates for other users to fill out.

48. HOW CAN I SELECT THE ENTIRE SHEET?

There are two ways.

a) Click on this symbol. This is the fastest way.

b) Start in A1. Then, Press Ctrl + Shift + Down Arrow, then press Right arrow.

49. HOW TO ADJUST COLUMN WIDTH QUICKLY

This is our starting point with different widths:

a) If you want all columns to be the same width. Select all columns, then change the width of just one of them:

b) If you want all columns to have the minimum possible width based on the content of each column. Select all of them and double-click on any of the cell separators:

50. HOW CAN I INSERT MANY ROWS/COLUMNS EFFICIENTLY?

Let's imagine you need to insert 10, 20, or 30 rows/columns for whatever reason. Going one by one takes time and kills your motivation. In our example we want to insert three rows between rows 1 and 2. Two ways of doing it:

	A
1	50
2	30
3	15
4	34
5	87

	A
1	50
2	
3	
4	
5	30
6	15
7	34
8	87

a) Using the mouse: select rows 4, 3 and 2 (select within the grey area where the row numbers are). Then if you have "insert row" in your quick-access ribbon (see tip #17), click on it or use its shortcut. Otherwise, right-click and "Insert".

b) Using the keyboard: select cell A2. Press Shift while using the arrows to select the range A2:A4. While the Shift key is pressed, press Space (this shortcut selects the entire row). Now, right-click and "Insert".

51. EXCEL DELETES LEADING ZEROS, HOW TO AVOID IT

Your spreadsheet stores telephone and credit card numbers. By default, Excel removes leading zeroes, which can create problems. Here are three options to avoid it:

a) Type an apostrophe (') before the number. Don't worry, lookup functions like VLOOKUP will ignore the apostrophe.

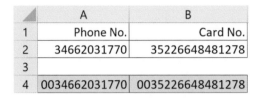

b) Use custom formats for each column (see tip #10). Knowing that credit cards have 16 numbers, you would use sixteen zeroes.

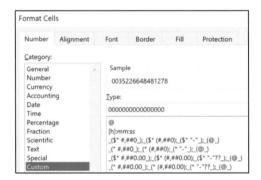

c) You can also choose "Text" as the format for your column, but this can cause issues with lookup functions, so I do not recommend it.

52. THE STATUS BAR IS YOUR BEST FRIEND

It is found on the bottom right of the spreadsheet. For quick analysis or calculations, take advantage of the status bar, where Excel shows different calculations and metrics based on the data you are currently selecting. You can customize it by right-clicking on it.

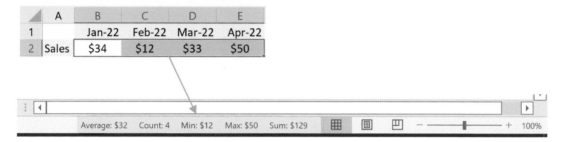

53. HOW TO KEEP ALL TEXT IN ONE CELL

Depending on the design of your spreadsheet you might be interested in having all text in just one cell. Select the cell where the text (A1 below) is and then, within "Home", click on [ab cↄ Wrap Text]   "Wrap Text"

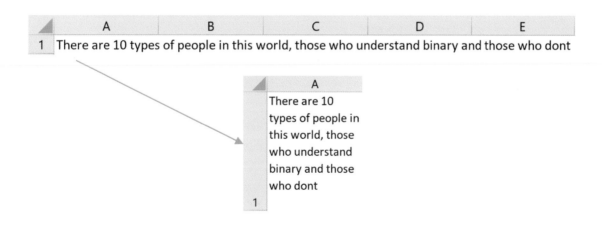

54. CAN I ADD A HYPERLINK IN A CELL?

Select the cell where you want the link, right click and select "Hyperlink…" or "Link" in newer versions of Excel. Then enter the link in the "Address" field and click OK.

55. HOW TO CREATE A SLICER TO FILTER A PIVOT TABLE?

Slicers are buttons that help you filter Pivot Tables (see tip #6). Charts whose data comes from pivot tables update automatically as you filter data. Therefore, this makes slicers a great tool to create interactive dashboards in Excel. This is because you can leave your pivot tables in a different tab as the backend, while having slicers and charts in your main tab. One slicer can filter more than one pivot table/chart.

Select your pivot table and then, within the PivotTable ribbon, click on Insert Slicer. Select what field of the table you want to use the slicer for and click OK.

Insert Slicer

There are many YouTube videos on how to create cool dashboards in Excel using slicers.

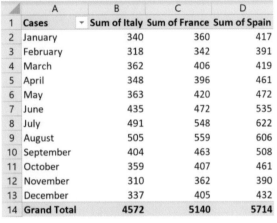

Cases	Sum of Italy	Sum of France	Sum of Spain
January	340	360	417
February	318	342	391
March	362	406	419
April	348	396	461
May	363	420	472
June	435	472	535
July	491	548	622
August	505	559	606
September	404	463	508
October	359	407	461
November	310	362	390
December	337	405	432
Grand Total	4572	5140	5714

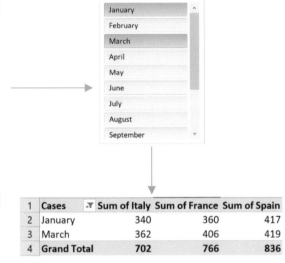

Cases	Sum of Italy	Sum of France	Sum of Spain
January	340	360	417
March	362	406	419
Grand Total	702	766	836

56. EXTRACT UNIQUE VALUES FROM A LIST (if you have Microsoft 365, use the "UNIQUE" function).

Sometimes we need the list of unique records within a table to work with them without a Pivot Table (tip #18) being the best solution. And sometimes we also need this list to update automatically as we add records. How do we do it?

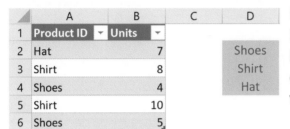

Enter the below formula in D2 and drag it down. **Do not be intimidated by how long it is because it is just one long formula duplicated to cover different scenarios within an IF statement.**

=IF(IFERROR(LOOKUP(2,1/(COUNTIF($D$1:D1,SalesTable[Product ID])=0),SalesTable[Product ID]),"")="","",LOOKUP(2,1/(COUNTIF($D$1:D1,SalesTable[Product ID])=0),SalesTable[Product ID]))

Let's build it step by step:

1. COUNTIF($D$1:D1,SalesTable[Product ID])
2. (COUNTIF($D$1:D1,SalesTable[Product ID])=0)
3. 1/(COUNTIF($D$1:D1,SalesTable[Product ID])=0)
4. LOOKUP(2,1/(COUNTIF($D$1:D1,SalesTable[Product ID])=0), SalesTable[Product ID])
5. IFERROR(LOOKUP(2,1/(COUNTIF($D$1:D1,SalesTable[Product ID])=0),SalesTable[Product ID]),"")
6. IF(IFERROR(LOOKUP(2,1/(COUNTIF($D$1:D1,SalesTable[Product ID])=0),SalesTable[Product ID]),"")="","",LOOKUP(2,1/(COUNTIF($D$1:D1,SalesTable[Product ID])=0),SalesTable[Product ID]))

1. It'll show an array of 1s or 0s depending on how many times D1 shows up in the ProductID column of my table. D1 must contain a name that will <u>never</u> show up in the ProductID column so choose wisely (in my case: "Unique values"). Note I only locked the first cell of the range because I want this range to grow as I drag the formula down.

   o   This formula in D2 will show: {0,0,0,0,0,0,0}, while for instance in D3 would be {0;0;0;1;0;1}

2. For each result it will show TRUE if they equal zero, otherwise FALSE: in D2: {TRUE;TRUE;TRUE;TRUE;TRUE;TRUE}. In D3: {TRUE;TRUE;TRUE;FALSE;TRUE;FALSE}. Remember that TRUE = 1, and FALSE = 0.

3. Therefore, if now in D2 we do 1/{TRUE;TRUE;TRUE;TRUE;TRUE;TRUE} = {1;1;1;1;1;1}. For reference, in D3 the result would be {1;1;1;#DIV/0!;1;#DIV/0!} because there were two FALSE (equivalent to dividing 1 by 0 → error). **We are causing these errors on purpose**. We have found "Shoes" already by the time our formula is in D3. Consequently, our COUNTIF formula shows 1s in positions 4th and 6th {0,0,0,1,0,0,1} like in the table. These two 1s don't equal zero, so they show up as FALSE, and FALSE equals zero. Then, 1 divided by these zeroes show the two errors we see above. What this means is that these 2 records from the table won't be considered when looking up values in the next step. In other words, you extract that record just once and then **you force the formula to show errors** so that you don't keep getting that name anymore, ending up with a list of unique records (our goal).

4. The LOOKUP formula looks for number "2" **intentionally** because this number is greater than any of the possible results from the previous step (all were either 1 or #DIV/0!). By looking for number "2" we force the formula to search through the end of the column. Because it will never find a "2", it will go back up and take the first "1" it finds. That's why it picks "Shirt" in D3 as the second result. The third argument of the formula (SalesTable[Product ID]) indicates which column (adjacent or not) it will pick the result from; in our case, after finding a result, it picks the result from the same column, but you could've chosen column SalesTable[Units] if necessary.

5. You can drag this formula all the way to the end of the worksheet. However, once you extract the full list of unique values, all the results from your LOOKUP formula will be #DIV/0! errors. Therefore, because of this, you add an IFERROR, which will show a blank when you don't have any more unique values left to be extracted.

6. IF the IFERROR shows a blank, then show a blank too. Otherwise, go with the result from the LOOKUP formula.

I agree that this formula is not easy or intuitive, but it's great to understand the logic of how formulas work in Excel. Now you know that you can create errors on purpose as a strategy to get to the solution you are looking for!

57. RANDOM LIST OF NAMES. HOW CAN I SORT ALPHABETICALLY? (In Microsoft 365, use the "SORT" function)

Using the results from tip #56 as a start point, now you want to sort this list alphabetically without manually using the Excel function "Sort & Filter". Check out this cool functionality of the formula COUNTIF.

The first thing I did is to transform this list into an Excel table using Ctrl+T. This way the results automatically update if the length of the list changes over time. I also changed the header "Unique values" and named it just "Values" for simplicity (when working with Excel tables, have 1-word headers if possible). Then, I added 3 helper columns:

- **Position** → whose formula is =COUNTIF([Values],"<="&[@Values]). For each value ([@Values]) in column A, give me the <u>relative position</u> within the entire [Values] column of the table.

- **1toN** → No formula, just an ascendent list from 1 to "n" being "n" the number of unique values in column A.

- **Sorted** → =INDEX([Values],MATCH([@1toN],[Position],0)). Lookup formula that helps us sort the values.

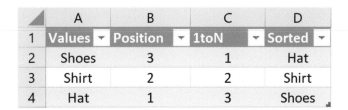

	A	B	C	D
1	Values	Position	1toN	Sorted
2	Shoes	3	1	Hat
3	Shirt	2	2	Shirt
4	Hat	1	3	Shoes

58. FIND SOLUTIONS TO ANY PROBLEM ON GOOGLE

I am an Excel autodidact. Most of the knowledge I have acquired comes from Google as I had to figure out how to solve problems in my professional career in Finance. They say that *the best coders are the best googlers*!

Depending on what type of business you support, your Excel needs will be different. However, no matter what you do, I can assure you that you are not the first person in the world having an extremely specific problem that needs to get solved in Excel. If you do not know how to solve it, go out there and look up that specific issue. I ended up teaching Excel to friends and colleagues, and always say this: *you can do anything you want in Excel*.

First, Google it (by the way, most of what you see in this guide coincides with the most looked up Excel questions on Google). Sometimes you might have to search multiple times when you are not sure of what you need exactly.

Second, check the titles of the articles that show up in the search results and open them in new tabs if you feel they could be answering your question. Do not look at them just yet, though. Keep looking and open more tabs until you have three or four.

Third, check those three or four tabs to see if the answer is in any of them. The key of opening several tabs is that sometimes the answer is in the combination of what you found in two or more of those tabs.

See below some of the best places to find solutions for Excel problems:

- Google – I always start here.

- StackOverflow.com – Very technical folks. You can post a question and get an answer very quickly.

- Reddit – Another great place to post questions, though your work computer might be blocking this site.

- Exceljet.net; excelforum.com; mrexcel.com; and YouTube for extra details.

Finally, the support.microsoft.com page usually shows up high in the Google results. However, for some reason it almost never has great answers. It goes very much by the book like if you read the Excel user guide.

59. HOW CAN I REFERENCE THE NAME OF MY TAB?

Sometimes we name our tabs in a specific way, i.e., "Week 25" to describe that the data it contains is from the 25th week of the year. The next week we update the name of the tab to "Week 26", and so on every week. To save time, how can we reference the tab name in our calculations so that we don't need to update for the current week anywhere else?

In this example we know our year-to-date (YTD) sales and want to calculate a sales per week ratio using the tab's name as the source for the number of weeks. The formula in B2 to reference the tab's name is =MID(CELL("filename",B2),FIND("]",CELL("filename",B2))+1,31).

	A	B
1	YTD Sales	$ 60,400
2	Period	Week 26
3	Sales per week	$ 2,323

It combines formulas MID, CELL, and FIND. As shown on the right, the formula CELL can return many of the properties of a cell: its color, type, row, and… filename. The filename property is what we are looking for here:

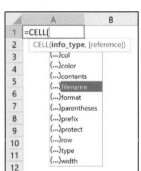

If my tab is called "Week 26" and in cell B2 I only enter =CELL("filename",B2), the result I get is "C:\Users\javier\Desktop\[Exceltips.xlsm]Week 26". It is the full path for each cell like if you were referencing it from another workbook. Note it says "Week 26" at the end, which is what we are looking for.

The formula FIND looks for specific text, in this case "]", which comes right before "Week 26".

As shown in tip #2, the function MID returns as many characters as you want from a text given the text itself, a starting point, and the number of characters you want to extract after the starting point.

-   The first CELL formula gives us the entire text from which we will extract.

-   FIND combined with CELL gives us the starting point: exactly one character after (+1) the "]" character.

-   The third argument of the MID formula is the number of characters. Why 31? Because a tab can only have as many as 31 characters, so this way you make sure you pull whatever name you chose for you tab.

By the way, the formula in B3 is =B1/RIGHT(B2,LEN(B2)-5), which uses the trick from tip #2 (VALUE function). It recalculates no matter if the number of weeks is a single digit or two.

60. WHAT QUARTER DOES THIS DATE CORRESPOND TO?

You have monthly financials and want to assign a quarter to each month. To find out the quarter and year "nQYY" you could use nested IF functions (see tip #7), but also this formula (example for cell B1):

=INT((MONTH(B2)-1)/3)+1&"Q"&RIGHT(YEAR(B2),2). The key to this formula is remembering that the INT function rounds down to the integer (see tip #42). We divide the result of (MONTH(B2)-1) by 3 so that the result shows always the same decimals for the first, second and third month of each quarter:

First month = n.0000   //   Second month = n.3333   //   Third month = n.6666

Now we apply the INT function to those results, getting the integer n. Next, we add 1 to that integer, and this gives us the number of the quarter we are looking for (1, 2, 3 or 4). To finish, we use "&" to concatenate the letter "Q" and the year, which we source using functions RIGHT and YEAR (tip #2).

	A	B	C	D	E	F	G	H	I	J	K	L	M
1		1Q22	1Q22	1Q22	2Q22	2Q22	2Q22	3Q22	3Q22	3Q22	4Q22	4Q22	4Q22
2		Jan-22	Feb-22	Mar-22	Apr-22	May-22	Jun-22	Jul-22	Aug-22	Sep-22	Oct-22	Nov-22	Dec-22
3	Sales	$1,136	$1,002	$ 702	$1,907	$1,904	$1,035	$ 936	$ 802	$ 502	$1,707	$1,704	$ 835

61. MACRO TO PICK THE COLOR OF A CELL AND USE IT ON ANOTHER ONE

Imagine that each quarter you receive a different palette of colors and that the background of dozens of cells must now match that new palette of colors. How do you do it automatically to avoid changing the color of all tables manually? You can use the code below.

Below, we have our new palette of colors in cell A1, and the range we need to update is B3:C3.

Note the "1" in the code. The code below works for changing just one color, but if your new palette of colors includes more than one, duplicate the structure of each section of the code replacing "1" by 2, 3, 4…

```
Sub colors()

Dim HEXcolor1 As String
Dim RGBcolor1 As String
Dim RGBcolor12 As String
Dim RGBcolor13 As String

'Get each RGB color of the background of the cell
HEXcolor1 = Right("000000" &
Hex(Worksheets("Sheet1").Range("A1:A1").Interior.Color), 6)
RGBcolor1 = CInt("&H" & Right(HEXcolor1, 2))
RGBcolor12 = CInt("&H" & Mid(HEXcolor1, 3, 2))
RGBcolor13 = CInt("&H" & Left(HEXcolor1, 2))

'Add that background color to another range
Worksheets("Sheet1").Range("B3:C3").Interior.Color = RGB(RGBcolor1,
RGBcolor12, RGBcolor13)

End Sub
```

62. USING POWER QUERY TO IMPORT FILES FROM OUTLOOK TO EXCEL

You sell peaches in South Carolina, and every day at 8:00am you receive 30 requests from customers who want to buy from you. Each customer sends you a spreadsheet, and all spreadsheets have the same format. How can you aggregate all requests in Excel with one click to know very quickly how much you are going to sell? See below how to do this in just a few seconds. Doing this manually would take a long time and would increase the risk for errors.

1. Open your Outlook inbox and create a folder called "Sales", where all requests from your customers will go.
2. In Power Query, create a New Query / From Online Services / Exchange Online
3. Enter your email address and click OK.
4. Right click on "Mail" / Edit
5. Add a text filter to the first column (Folder Path) to equal the name of the shared inbox or folder you created. If you created a subfolder within your normal Inbox and called it "Sales", your text filter should be "\Inbox\Sales\".
6. Scroll to the right until you find the "Attachments" column. Click on "Table".
7. Add a text filter to the second column (Extension) to equal ".xslx". At this point you should see all Excel files stored in that folder.
8. Scroll to the right until you find the "AttachmentContent" column and hit the button with the two arrows pointing down.
9. Select the tab within the spreadsheet where your customers entered their orders. Then hit OK.
10. At this point all your customers' orders are aggregated in just one place. Now it is a matter of formatting the appended results to make them look exactly the way we want.
11. Close & Load. The first time, Excel will create a new tab containing the resulting table from the query.
12. Using that table, create a pivot table (see tip #6) to show metrics such as total sales, or total units sold.

Optional: after step #12, you can create a button (see tip #7) to refresh both the query and the pivot table in case you received additional offers in your inbox, or on the next day. The VBA code to refresh the query would be just:

```
Private Sub CommandButton1_Click()
ThisWorkbook.RefreshAll

End Sub
```

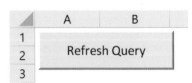

63. HOW MANY WEEKS ENDING ON A FRIDAY ARE THERE IN A MONTH?

Some businesses close their month on the last Friday of the month, while others use the last day of the month. If you work in a company that uses the first method and want to calculate ratios such as units sold per week for a given month, how do you do it? The formula you need in D2 is a little long… No need to memorize it, just copy and paste it. =((EOMONTH(B2,0)+1-WEEKDAY(EOMONTH(B2,0)+1-6))-(EOMONTH(A2,0)+1-WEEKDAY(EOMONTH(A2,0)+1-6)))/7

This formula subtracts the date of the last Friday in July and the date of the last Friday in June. Then it divides by 7 to get the number of weeks between the last Friday of both months.

The key is understanding how it works. As you see in tip #11, EOMONTH(B2,0) would give you the last day of the month (July 31st); and if you add up 1 EOMONTH(B2,0)+1, you get the first day of the following month (August 1st).

Now a new function, WEEKDAY. The only argument of this function is a date, like B2. Based on what day of the week that date falls on, it will give you a number from 1 to 7, where 1 is Sunday, and 7 is Saturday. If the date is blank, it also returns 7. The next part of the formula WEEKDAY(EOMONTH(B2,0)+1-6) calculates the number of days you need to go back from that first day of the month (August 1st, Monday) to the previous Friday July 29th (3 days). Now you subtract this number to August 1st to get the last Friday in July: July 29th.

You would do the same thing for June, getting June 24th. Then, July 29th minus July 24th equals 35 days. Next, divide by 7 to get the number of weeks between the last Friday of both months = 5 weeks.

	A	B	C	D
1	Dates			Number of weeks ending on Friday in July?
2	Jun-22	Jul-22		5

Note the "6" in the formula. If instead of the last Friday you need the last Monday or Sunday, use the guide below.

	A	B	C	D	E	F	G	H
1	Weekday	1	2	3	4	5	6	7
2	Last…	Sunday	Monday	Tuesday	Wednesday	Thursday	Friday	Saturday

64. QUESTIONS OR FEEDBACK? CONTACT ME

My goal was to create a guide that responds the most frequently asked questions about Excel to help as many people as possible. I used Answerthepublic.com to produce a list, and then added some more content based on my own experience working with Excel. I have used these tips many times in my professional career as a Financial Analyst, and I have seen colleagues and friends using them as well. I did my best to explain concepts concisely, and I am aware that a comprehensive guide would have hundreds of pages. Everything is original content and I hope it helps you.

If you want to contact me:

LinkedIn – linkedin.com/in/javiersz/

Twitter – @jsanzsz

E-mail – excel.tips.contact@gmail.com

Thank you!

Printed in Great Britain
by Amazon

15655187R00036